Transcontinental Delay

Transcontinental Delay

by

Simon van Schalkwyk

DRYAD PRESS

People! Read Poetry

Transcontinental Delay

Dryad Press (Pty) Ltd
Postnet Suite 281, Private Bag X16 Constantia, 7848,
Cape Town, South Africa
www.dryadpress.co.za
business@dryadpress.co.za

Cover design and typography: Stephen Symons
Editor: Michèle Betty
Copy Editor: Helena Janisch

Set in 9.5/14pt Palatino Linotype

First published in Cape Town by Dryad Press (Pty) Ltd, 2021

Visit www.dryadpress.co.za to read more about all our books and to buy them.
You will also find features, links to author interviews and news of author
events. Follow our social media platforms on Instagram and Facebook to be
the first to hear about our new releases.

ISBN 978-1-990992-28-5 (Print)
ISBN 978-1-990992-29-2 (Electronic)

Dryad Press is supported by the Government of South Africa through the
National Arts Council of South Africa (an Agency of the Department of Arts &
Culture), whose assistance is gratefully acknowledged.

for Jennifer Malec

CONTENTS

Inner Workings

I

It was a place of scrap,
of bits and parts.

In the disappearing world of their garage,
they worked together, almost wordlessly.

Bob would set some Holden panel van's heart
to beating, with pliers, wrench and oil.

Lyle studied the anatomy of clocks, their inner workings,
the gears that made them tick.

Spread carefully across the dark matter
of folded velvet, their bright wheels and cogs

were space junk, defunct satellites,
mere debris. Some way away,

at their bare junkyard's edge,
a spooked mare bolted through an open field.

Bob would flick his grease-flecked fringe to glance
at my passing shadow in the door.

But Lyle would barely raise his head, bowed close
to the workbench, where he winked at watches.

Wearing his Kruder eye loupe, he seemed less
my grandfather than some high priest of time.

II

To enter their orbit
was to be arraigned by an older world.

Drifting through girders of light, even the dust motes
had weight, reliable substance, gravity.

Like the last Indo-European phoneme
that still harboured traces of the ancestry

of all our language, Bob's gone for good.
Lyle left behind an Elgin hunter case,

and the old eye loupe with its metal spool
that gripped the skull.

Peering through the mare's nest of its lens,
I see the worn teeth of wheels and tourbillons,

escapements, complications,
the markings on a white, Masonic dial:

tools by which to set
unsettled time.

I

South (the Cape)

(1977–2001)

A Question for the South Atlantic Ocean

~ *South African Navy Festival, East Dockyard, Simonstown*

It happens to the best of us—
days come and go.
It is summer again—I remember;
it is new as yesterday.

All along the beachfront
crowds gather and disperse,
parades go by,
the sound of a seaside Sunday
bought and sold.

Mistakes are made, or happen.
Dogs slip the leash, sailboats capsize,
children are lost and found—
across the bay, pockets of cloud
drift and disperse, like thoughts.

Something is in the air,
the suspended cross of an aircraft,
contrails, cirrus, space.
My friends are somewhere.

Meanwhile, the ocean
ducks and falls like a penguin.
You ask the time and I tell you—
it is late, we have missed the hour
of embarkation.

Somewhere in town, colonial statues
disclose their laundry of shadows.
Across the square,
the window-blinds are drawn.

Cast

I

The narrow path is grazed with sand-swept grass,
sun-bleached driftwood, camel-thorn, parched aloe.

Hissing melkbos deadens as they pass
palindromes of spoor where nothing follows.

Things trail into nowhere, with no clear
end or initiation. The beveled dunes

are distant, suffer the worst of wind shear.
They should get there soon.

II

And then, the lighthouse—long abandoned twin
casting antic light across the black Atlantic.

The morning sky unspools, a single thread
uncoiled from snarl and loop and knot,

guided by the eye, baited and hooked,
cast into this salt-swept, wind-swept, sharp-rocked gully.

III

They still call it gut, these tensile lines
angled against limit, twitching, dragged by tides.

They bend into the catch—*steenbras, geelbeck, kabeljou, galjoen,*
a guitarfish, gasping on feldspar:

tiger-eyed, chatoyant, moon-mouthed,
abrasively skinned.

IV

A man hauls in a small, pale-bellied shark,
cuts the line some way from a hooked gill,

grasps the tailfin, lifts, and then brings down
the denticled body hard against shale.

Everyone pays witness to the murder:
these men; the distant boy who walked away;

those children, looking on as mother gathers
limpets and periwinkles for the pot.

Infauna

Cloudless before sunset, a day without fog,
clear as white handkerchiefs waving away
ships and present commitments.
An apostrophe also for the duneless future.

Who wades, shin-deep, between sculpins,
silver and quick, in the pellucid shallows
of the Kromme? What are these murmuring flues,
submerged corridors, enclosed labyrinths,

suggesting a deeper habitat? Inter-tidal plateau,
crystalline floodplain, freshwater, salt,
stray aquarelle of urchin, isolated hydra, detached
polyp, sessile and repeating: the ghost crab's lair.

Black River Catchment

I

I have never seen the Neva,
but I have heard

it is a black hiss, black
as home's Black River,

but with a wave like a medusa.
There is no comparison

but that the Black is still
and smooth as tourmaline.

Here, the Black tongue sibilates
from Arderne, sinks into karst,

canalised, seeps
through riparian rubbish.

Our Lady, schorl-faced hyacinth girl,
sleeps towards a desolate and empty sea.

II

I have never seen the Seine,
but I have heard

it is an old egotist,
dreaming of the blue ghosts

of kingfishers.
There is no comparison—I,

have never been one
to make things happen.

I, the undersigned,
exact as the flamingo,

stilted in fading light,
filter the Black brine.

Drive

Cue hailstorm,
ice scudding the windscreen,

wind shaking the car
the way a dog shakes a child.

This is us, working through it;
edging through floodplain,

an hour's drive out of the city,
and now this, now this.

You always see it coming:
a distant photograph of rain;

the dulling of daylight
into storm light; anvils

of Highveld arcus
boring into the horizon;

the sky arriving like a god.
And *oh*, we remark, arrowing

into it, *here it comes.*
And then, *Oh, God, it's here.*

Foxglove

~ Orange Free State, Oranje

This is where they go when they are tired of the sea —
that interminable wash and motion,

the bleached blues of worried beaches,
sandplains shimmering against the eye

until all sight becomes whitewash.
Here, in the space between wind pump and wheat field,

where flatlands are overflown with quarreling sparrows,
the still lives of silo, mill and thresher

remain unpainted, and the Cape Dutch house
sets a Calvinistic jaw against the hills.

This is their soul's country:
fenced-in-farmlands, hay bales with long hidden needles,

the asystasia running to black frost,
and wind pump after wind pump barely waving.

Lodger

Years later, you return there, to that place above the pines,
to be surprised again by the tone of water,
the unnatural cold of cliff-sides,
and you remember how you had once thought
that the stones were weeping.

What is it about this place that makes time seem unremarkable,
that considers you the way a child would,
having lifted a stone to study
the curious ecology that lives there
before losing interest?

You think about the uncanny precision of your horoscope,
or how a writer pauses to read what has been written
before deciding to erase it all.
Funny how things change.
Yet still, the twilight will surge with romance

like candles during a blackout,
and you will struggle happily along,
watching the cooling towers billow with assurance,
or observing a monumental windmill,
though your mind will be elsewhere.

Why do such details impress themselves upon you?
For whom have these signs been planted,
and who puzzles them,
effaced by weather or general disrepair,
back into meaning? You stand there, unable to read,

but less anxious for having located the signpost.
Others had been there at least.
They must have seen what you have seen,
thought what you have thought,
or been who you had been.

Pyriscence

There comes a time on walks
into the mountain when speech and birdsong
fall far off the cliffs.

You stop to study prints in furrowed gravel,
thinking that the persistent hiss
of insects—how it recurs—

has always seemed to you the sound of heat.
A locust clacks hard wings
through husks of honeypot,

charred by last year's arson, to these effigies
of blackened candelabra,
and a low smoke of mauve

blurs the contours, upward, to the cave
you hope to reach by noon,
to see again the names

chalked across cave walls, the drenched mattresses,
wrecked deckchairs, and the dead,
skeletal blossoms of umbrellas.

Pearl and Carnelian

The path inclines, gently, to a rise, and they follow the sloping gradients
hinting at a purer geometry while never quite asserting an ideal line.
It was all traffic at first, then broken silence—scrape of boot on gravel,

hushed shuffle across the gravel track—and then, typically, an oracle:
Great Dane black as pitch, a shimmering mirage, holding the hilltop
till called to heel by a man stamping at his reflection in pools of rainwater.

Later, they stare down a chasm where the stones wear furs—
emerald pelts of moss, turquoise scales of lichen, fungal plateaus
drummed by water coursing from the canopy. Pearl and carnelian

glinting in the *komorebi*. Here, the stone pines whirl their pointed roots
amid swamps of eukaryotic life, deadwood and vine, glistening darkly there.
They stop near a rock face steeped with rain, where the call of a bird

traveling toward them traps itself in crags and echoes quickly away.
Pearl and carnelian. The bird sends out song after song
after its twin. Pearl and carnelian. Song after song. Poor bird.

Another Man

Forget me. I am never coming back—
tomorrow I will be another man.

Already, now, I wear a stranger's face,
and I have carried someone else's hands

ever since I threw my voice away
and buried my old body in the sand.

If I return, half altered, from this place,
where I grow less familiar with each day,

I should admit that you are what I've lacked—
if I come back. But I will not come back.

II

West Country

(2002–2004)

Christmas Steps

When it's cold like this, and winds pelt the sky,
I remember Bristol, how different it was, and colder
despite the absence of these winds—
the tantrum of a petulant Cape storm.

There, the cold keeps its temper,
looks through you, as if you were a ghost,
as if it knows that your days there are numbered.
Then, losing interest, it snows,

and Knyfesmyth vanishes with you as you walk,
plaintive footsteps echoing through Old Town,
as your doppelgänger stalks behind you.
Someone will replace you. Someone does.

Latitudes

The fireworks begin,
randomly, amid distant
persuasions of star

and satellite. They
wink—lemon, coral, chartreuse—
between ink-stained tree-

line and a backcloth
of noctilucent cirrus.
Pleasant enough now,

but soon, the threadbare
room again, the study of
certain attitudes,

idle chatter
in the dorm kitchenette with
Ricky, a neuro-

scientist from Seoul.
Midway through a game of chess
(endgame, knights) he says,

Still, we do not know
what is memory, then stares
to one side, his glazed

eye falling on dark
windows spun with stillicides.
In my room, I read:

Questions of Travel
and *Geography III*. Not
all stars are fixed in

West Country. Bishop
in Petrópolis shares a
southern latitude.
-

Cabot Tower

~ Bristol

Cabot wrote, *the land of America was found by the Merchants of Bristow*
in a shippe of Bristowe, called the Mathew.

En route to China, via the phantom isle of Hy-Brazil, they made landfall,
laughably, in Nova Scotia.

It is noted that the crew found *a trail … inland, a fire … and … a stick a half*
yard long pierced at both ends carved and painted with brazil.

Imagine them: hoary men with icicles for beards, sea-salt crusting their
coldsores, huddled beneath slick sealskins, bearskins, sheepskins.

They carried their abattoir with them, curing the meat with salt, anointing
themselves with fat.

Latchkey

The reader will often see a particular word, idea or image lifting the latch on the next …

— Stephen James, *The Tabla Book of New Verse*

This was in Wales. We had hiked our way
from the city to more rural parts,
where sheep roamed suburban roads, pock-marked
with their pellets, pungent with their smell.

Our map indicated a defunct railway
and a waterfall, something to walk towards,
so we began to walk there, in the rain.
The road gave way to gravel, stones, then mud,

until the post and rail that we had followed
for a thousand lands or so slowly fell away
at a place where, as the bark-rot showed,
it must have rained more often than elsewhere.

We came to the crossing around midday,
after field upon empty, mist-drenched field,
and began to climb a path that rose
in a spiral around an untrammeled core

of gorse, shattered timber, weather-worn stone.
In the shadows of this wild recess, I saw
a ram, wool-wet, hooves tapping at the plinth,
watchful as a sentry before a door.

We were not wanted, nor unwanted, there,
but foreign enough for it to watch
with a dark intelligence our passing:
it would not lift the latch to let us in.

The Menai Strait

Following roundpoles until these vanished,
we walk, in rain as soft as radio-waves,
where the whistling sheep and braying winds

conduct arias for being almost lost.
Think of it as an old broadcast, she said,
half-heard through skirls and whispers

of some delinquent frequency. To become
accustomed to all this weather takes some tuning,
some calibrated gentleness of feeling, as thieves

set their stethoscopes to the safe, listening,
until something finally clicks.
Try another channel, and I did, peering

at planes and vectors, inhaling knots of ley,
mists, gorse, and brushing my gloves across
another drystone wall. Funny:

the mute air and stone, yellow snags of wool
a bit like crying, the type of ugly rain called *sunshower* ...
Let's see where this will lead.

Hay-on-Wye

~ for Katherine, David and James

I

We drive there on a whim in someone's car.
From the back seat, through my misted window,
I peer at hedgerows: the rank and file that guard
wide reserves of private, English, meadow.

These flicker, on occasion, through rough breaks
of unclipped brush where great West Country buck
must once have broken through. I see them shake
rustic antlers at onrushing trucks.

They must have had no chance. But there are roads
less Roman, that follow the brooks and rills
forgetfully, in rambling fashion, to roam
thoughtless into narrows, across bridges that spill

over millponds, well known by local names
and leading to market towns like Hay-on-Wye.
This is where the pony shakes its mane
against the black fly and the mayfly

and the Welsh Marches meet West Country brogues.
Here, lane leads onto lane less by design
than luck, mischance, the unlikely logic of an eclogue.
It is too cosy (we are too unkind).

II

This is the 'town of books': we see them rise
in staggered stacks, high as any hedgerow,
and cast our eyes across their damaged spines,
lift half-damp leaves stained dirty, haystack yellow,

to check the prices penciled in the endpapers.
I find Yevtushenko's *Selected Poems*
wondering how he slipped across Siberia
to end up here, so very far from 'home'.

In the Russian way, he says, *dancing and weeping
to songs I am unable to translate.*
A poet's game: some music for some meaning—
glacial lakes for bits of chalk and slate.

The sun sets. The stacks appear to catch
fire, as we gather in a hall
to hear poets from elsewhere lift the latch
to let the last light in—to taste the ash.

Future Scenarios

Off the small stone terraced stair, outside a green door, making the most of the Bristol snow—this is the first time I have experienced snow: *skift* and *onding*, *firn* and *sposh*, the clear black ice—I light another cigarette, imagining likely future scenarios.

...

I

I never leave. Eventually, I marry a perfectly charming Englishwoman (Cornish extraction), someone I met at a party. I am still young enough to be invited to parties and to feel like going to them. I mill about, sipping beer. Urged to take a toke, I take a toke. I join a small circle of strangers who, I learn, have a shared enthusiasm for Belle and Sebastian's *Tigermilk*. There is something almost Christian about their praise. A close friend of mine keeps talking about the 'pear-shaped' woman on the far side of the room. He is drinking obsessively, beginning to break out in a sweat, and asking me if she's looking our way. She isn't. Nevertheless, he imagines that there is something between them. Weeks pass, but things do not work out. One evening, years later, I find myself sharing a cab with her as we make our way home after a chance meeting at a performance of Malcolm Arnold's *Four Cornish Dances*. She is one of the violinists in the orchestra. *So many dangerous entries*, she says, wide-eyed, before inviting me to another, different party. I barely remember the context, but, in the future, we tell our friends—our new friends—how we shared a drunken cab and spent a night trying to have any kind of sex at all, and failing. It is because we can never forget this tragedy that binds us—in shame or some sense of comic futility—to one another. *Remember,* I say, *how I held your hair while you vomited—puaaaaagh!—into the latrine. That's how I knew it was love.*

II

On the night-bus back home, I catch a glimpse of two blue-rinsed women walking a dog in the dead spaces of the London Orbital. They stare back at me, their eyes glowing a bright gray, like Midwich Cuckoos. A few days later, homeland security realises that I have been surviving here, illegally—*I am an illegal alien now,* I think, when they eventually track me down—*I have never imagined myself this way until this precise moment, officer, when you leveled your accusation.* On a global scale, I guess, the English are essentially all Tory. But, for reasons unknown, a lassitude overcomes them—the police, I mean—and I am let off with a caution. Relieved, I head out into suburbia. It is early evening and hoodied boys on BMX bikes have tossed fireworks into another cherry-red post-office box, now burning freely. The fire brigade has finally come to Uxbridge. No one seems much concerned.

III

I never leave. But I never marry. Instead, I make a living working first at *Waterstones,* then at *Wetherspoons.* I am not indispensable to either outlet, but I come to think of them as 'families' and I divide my time and labour between them. We are all surprisingly comfortable with this arrangement. In my spare time, I pretend that I am writing a novel. I take long walks into the boring English countryside, persuading myself that it is deeply and importantly suffused with the weird and the eerie, that I am participating in *dérive*. Really, I am just finding words for describing what's there and what isn't there. It's better, of course, to refer to these country walks as exercises in *hauntology, situationism, psychogeographical mapping*. So this is what I say I do at parties and job interviews. But really, I am only biding time—running through the motions of life, copying others. For joy, I buy a few records at *Wanted* and *Rough Trade* or I take cheap trips to London by early-morning bus to see the Camden Market. An inexpensive pleasure: to walk through the open-air stalls rebuffing the desperate attentions of vendors hoping to shift other people's clothes. No one in London seems to be a Londoner. Before I head back, I usually have an uneven pint at *The World's End*, secretly assessing other people's tattoos and piercings, thinking about modifying my own body, wondering about their politics, and imagining what I would look like with a new face.

IV

I leave. Things are misty for a time, but then the mist clears. And then the mist returns, clears, returns … and so on. I become important enough to travel by air to European conferences on the subject of *Security*. Right now, I am somewhere over Eritrea or Gabon—countries I know little about but which, for reasons unknown, I suspect of being listed as zones of 'anthropogenic disaster'. Places frequented by *Medicins Sans Frontiers*. The airport I am traveling to—a Bentham-shaped specimen somewhere in beef-goulash Eastern Europe—has been destroyed by a meteor. We passengers do not know this. We travelers. We accept that our plane may disappear from radar, our green blip vanishing somewhere between airspaces, and that we will never be found, consigned to the annals of another aeronautical mystery. I consider this while dousing my face in a hot towel, enjoying the heat on my skin, feeling my pores opening and closing, like anemone. I am thinking about my next move: to sit here without agency, watching in-flight television. Later, the plane will enter a holding pattern, circling the sky in a tried and tested formation, above the rubble that used to be an airport, just like the end of Tom McCarthy's *Remainder*.

...

I flick my cigarette—presto—the snow ignites, and a small flame burns luminous emerald, like foxfire.

Black Swan

Exit the white door, light a cigarette—
the first of late afternoon.
The sun is relaxed,
and clouds flop over things,
as in the letters of Ezra Loomis Pound.

Linger at Pero's Bridge.
Rattle the locks of love and bondage,
wait for the black swan's arrival,
the outlying future.
Nothing yet, so I walk on, past *Society*,

and down Narrow Quay
to meet the lost man, Cabot,
plinthed before the Arnolfini.
My heart, like the portrait by Van Eyck,
is marriage and a dog—

fidelity, sable, ermine, silks.
Later, sitting alone in *The Old Duke*
with my pint of *Conquest*,
I write letters to nobody,
until the last call of *time*.

London Orbital

Mud and English heather line the fosse
from Heathrow all along the M25—northward,
where ice-green floes scud from the glacier
into thawing elsewheres. The future
is a warmer, less waterlogged diary.

Traffic looms through London fog and burns
incandescent pathways through the gloom—
another dark orbit for the coach
through culverts of mud and English heather.
I walk into an Arctic wind.

A streak of foxfur—tufts of foxfur snagged
on razor-wire are dislodged by the squall.
They tumble along beside the glacis,
urged politely, but firmly, to move on.
I turn to take one last look at the Shard.

Transcontinental Delay

They are waiting for you to come back.
You mull this over, chewing ramen absently.
The rooms are bathed in blank light, all the same.
Whatever home is, this could be it.

Outside, the light continues, day for night.
Look at them: vomiting and pissing in the street.
England—the foregone conclusion of Greece and Rome.
Civilizations in decline for the last two thousand years.

You will never find darkness here, a soft cocoon.
The swans beg for clemency; you give them bread.
All's even now, all square—please move along.
Down to the boathouses, where Chinese lanterns hang

like instruments for wind. Charms, moorings,
riverlights, the small plash of tossed money,
wavelets lapping waterproofed hulls.
Maybe things will be different in the morning

when dawnlight calls for excise, door to door.
Talk to me about latency. Tell me—
ignore the transcontinental delay.
I will wait for your mouth to arrive at my ear,

listening, in the meantime, to the meantime—
listening in, waiting for your voice to traverse
continents, via cables, undersea. This is the cost
of arrival—money for a few minutes of air.

III

South, Again (a Deadzone)

(2005–2014)

Curiosity CLXXV

a recovery from 'Love Letter to a University'
– Henk Rossouw

Waiting, while keys were found to long-locked storerooms,
we recovered treasures—a mandolin decorated with ivory
and snakeskin, a stuffed orangutan clutching a dead branch.
No one remembers why. I want what doesn't get seen,

what gets thrown away. Is the eucharist still the body
of Christ if it is nibbled by a rat? When does meaning
leave it? What becomes of it when its meaning is gone?
Look deeply into the glass eye. 175 years, 175 cabinets

filled with fascinating clutter. The effect is like stumbling
into the back room of a museum and discovering objects
that never go on display: a stiletto shoe with a bit of skull
stuck to the sharp heel; a whale's ear, the only memento

of a waterlogged vocation, and Giambattista Marino's
disembodied voice, arriving from C16th Naples: *Let him*
who does not know how to astonish go and work in the stables!
But what are we to make of these archaeological stones

set in an incubator? Or the delicate, papery row of blue crane
skulls set amid pipettes? A book of administrative records
from 1917 (stamped "confidential" in red ink) lies splayed
at a page revealing a squashed moth. These are amusing—

the umbrella used to fend off riot police, the veto against
blackness, the photograph of a usually austere novelist
begarbed in a cassock—hands clasped in prayer, the gold-leaf
replica of a woman's foot set against patriarchal statistics.

Elsewhere, the contents of a rudimentary hunting lodge
waits in a museum in Tromsø, raising the important question
of annihilation: 23 blue foxes, 36 reindeer, and 22 polar bears,
the heads of hunted nomads cast in plaster. Recovered treasures.

#Fallism

I

Like dissipating weather,
something has passed over
the still plazas
and arched colosseums—
the tilted shadow of the bird
outside the frame—
a contemplation.

II

What are we to make of it all,
especially now, when nothing
but the shards of another window
crisping like tinsel on brickwork
seems official?

III

Even the hills
have been occupied.
Can a twinkling chime
still be heard
over the manifestos?
Listen at an angle.

IV

Certain programmes leave me cold
and that's allowed—
to drift through a day
without being called to order
whatever disparate obsession
keeps me company.
Courting irrelevance, listlessly
engaged, I break off
appointments, by now,
so undramatically
they let me wear my used tuxedo
to the wake.

V

What shall we do tomorrow night?
How shall we commit and compromise?
Gather the plates,
sweep the art school floor.

Installations

I walk from the uncrowded station past the flower booth—
packing up—the entire city gathering its things into bundles,
tying them together with string, and carting them down Strand.
Last year's Christmas lights blink, looping across Adderley.

St. George's, crowdless as De Chirico, draws a scrap of news
over its shoulder and goes to sleep. Long begins to maunder,
and João Ferreira meets us on the corner of Hout, casting light
like cheap chardonnay all over someone's dress. *Don't Panic—*

A Million Trillion Gazillion—Take Me to Your Leader.
I step outside, away from trust fund chatter
to listen instead to the squabbling seagulls,

the vagrants muttering artlessly to themselves,
and in the distance, sirens—the last train out of town.
It is 2006. I am here, on the outside, looking out.

Je Suis Après l'Avant-Garde

The rehearsed gesture
as if they were winking at the future,
as if writing them this way rather than that
would be enough.

> It seemed so
> urgent to them;
>
> it was so urgent
> to them.

But the stakes were higher then,
weren't they?
Still capable of adding value to their play:
rules set out clearly enough to be easily broken;
lines drawn and crossed and then
entirely erased.

Significant consequences.

The Firs/Foundling's Island

~ for Peter Anderson

*It is only through personal contact that one can get a few glimpses into
the hidden depths of the primitive and childlike yet rich soul of the native,
and this soul is what I try to reflect in my pictures*
    – Irma Stern, *My Exotic Models*

I

The lurid colours and ugly, cult-like paintings:
here we have a Buli stool;
there, portraits from Zanzibar, the Congo, Dakar;
landscapes—the bay of Câmara De Lobos, Madeira;
Still Life with Antirrhinums from North Africa.
A degenerate house.

Half-bodied cinderblock women
are sequestered in the garden.

II

The magnet of exotica …

*brought in straight from the sea,
huge skites, small vivid-blue fish
with yellow stripes, silvery kinds,
red roman, enormous lobsters
as made of turquoise matrix,*

*phantastic huge turtles—
all come out of the tropical sea …*

III

Years later, others will shroud
the soldered Venus in a kanga.
Tentacles of ink spilled to account
for the unaccountable. It never
occurred to me; it has happened.
Elsewhere, the plinths stand empty.
Nothing gazes now at any hinterland.

Underneath the Paving Stones

I

This has been a long time coming.
The wait is over.
The paving stones
have finally been crowbarred from their moorings
and the crowds are surging.

Buses arrive, police arrive, helicopters arrive.
Flash-Bang. History in the making.
And look: someone has lost a shoe.
That can't be any good, but it is necessary.

II

Hey, wait up! We would like to join the gang.
It is a hot day, *chaleur*, as they say in France,
and we are heading for the beach. *Bon chance.*

But we are not in France,
and my heart is not in it.
It never is.
Perhaps there is another way
of looking at things.

Imago

~ for Sophy Kohler

You were neither cockroach nor *Mistkäfer*
but a beetle with wings beneath the shell.
Kafka called you *ungeheures Ungeziefer*
and though he once referred to you as *Insekt*,
he said you were not to be depicted,
meaning that no image should distract
from your essential lack of clarity.
Fitting, then, that you should be lost

somewhere between tongues: vermin, bug,
both miss the mark; you were the unclear,
the guest, the traveler roaming from house to house;
eternal stranger, rumour, Wandering Jew.
Unsurprising, then, that you were not surprised
by your *Verwandlung: Immer unheimlich, du.*

Preoccupations

An agent of state arrives
to dismantle underground dwellings
in the countryside.

People had literally
moved *into the land,*
only to be moved out again.

A way of saying: you cannot live here
—you cannot live anywhere—
you cannot live.

Saudades

~ in memory of Stephen Watson

Long after the sun descends (once more)
to the level of those stone pines, set askew

along the black ridge of the Old Mule path,
I lean in to read the sulcalised spines

of books in your lost library: *Watermark,*
Calligrammes and *Elegy for the Departure.*

The sea-wind withers, and I light the lamps,
staring out from the darksome sea-deck

and across the windblown bay, staring out
as far as Seal Island. *You look,* you once said,

like a refugee. I still remember.
Now, I set a flame to the hearth, uncork

the *Flagstone* and, with bread and cheese,
begin to read: Mr Cogito

still sends reports from his besieged city;
in late afternoon bedrooms and cafés,

empty but for *saudade*, Cavafy holds
a straw hat at an angle to his melancholy;

and, elsewhere, Miłosz remembers Wilnow
in alexandrines, very much like yours.

In the end, each letter is an entry
or an envoi in some other writer's diary.

Tableaux Vivants

A city square,
plumed with abandoned statues,
ossified feathers in the cap of State.

Obsolete cargo,
the green of Greece, discarded
in some vast, uncanny junkyard
for History, capital H.
Upper-case memories.

One sculpture,
the beaded ear of Johanna Six,
listens for paintings.
There are others—

    the sailor's dog,
    the drowned horse,
    a life-sized replica of the SS Waratah,
        sinking,
    tableaux vivants of 'Duke' Duquesne
        and Roosevelt hunting rhino.

And there, the visionary—
epaulettes and passenten
daubed in feral-pigeon spatter.

The *sieg heil* hand,
severed at the wrist,
is still missing.

Some say
it has been seen in the shrouded basements
of the National Gallery,
hovering over colonial landscapes and portraiture,
involved in random acts of restoration.

Bread and Roses

(I don't want to go,
    but they are waiting.)

So we walk, from the underground garage
where a *High Risk* security guard
sits on a milk-crate
listening to two-way radio static.

(Out,
    into the bright, polluted sunset.)

We are talking about something,
and I am listening
    and almost listening,
distracted by five men near the corner
struggling to lift a glass aquarium.

(I worry that the entire ordeal will end
badly.)

But then we're past them and at the corner,
where *Bread and Roses* used to be,
    now closed forever

(just like Socialism, I think, jazz,
and the ever-alarming future.)

But anyway,
we're past it now and moving
through the usuals pretending that *The Ant*
    is a Parisian café,

past *Miss Lonelyhearts*,
        open, but still unfinished

(like my own heart, I almost think,
        as if I were a poem by Frank O'Hara.)

When we arrive, it is too late.
I am no longer present enough to recall
        the names of my friends.

So I am relieved when someone else arrives,
        at last,
with her many boyfriends,
        and suddenly everyone is talking at the same time.

(Except,
        we are not all having the same conversation, are we?
We are not at all
        all present at the same time.)

IV

Floating Points

(2014–2020)

Sea Wall

Arriving, unmoored, they greet the foreshore
without preconceived assumptions.
Wearing other people's clothes,

they drag push-carts freighted with cardboard,
copper, scorched mattresses, a dead body.
I'm told they know the loaded docks,

the ferries of Maersk and Grindrod
emblems of an untouchable horizon.
On reclaimed land, in the shadow of a castle,

they burn rags, listening to the sea wall:
a threnody of tides and traffic, cargo.
I'm told this, knowing less, now, about city walking,

missing it: monoxide, crowds, the flower seller's booth,
my hard stare given unasked,
and walking into dead space, the concrete shade.

I am determined to get where I am going,
holding myself composed before the knife.
And if my heart stops beating, and I stop breathing,

if, for a second, I have died,
it will be for the good of relinquishing
replaceable cards, a phone that nobody calls.

Orpheline

~ Buenos Aires

These Rodins arrest me;
light fills the room and falls

on surface, into cavity
of pooled shadow.

I am almost in thrall
of *Despairing Youth and Child of Ugolino*,

*small floral souls raised out
of antique vases*, or

the *Assemblage: Fish Woman and Torso
of Iris on Foliated Plinth*.

I am especially drawn
to *Orpheline Alsacienne*,

egglike on her plinth, forlorn
and pale, marmoreal—

her forehead rests on a scarf
of marble quarried from Alsace-Lorraine.

Villa Miseria

I take a train from Quilmes to the city
and all I see are plastic rivers on fire—
marshlands, swamps, the future.

In Buenos Aires, I trade in currency—
the peso, and the black peso and the dollar.
I spend time reading Borges in the Borges library.

And then, suddenly, it is evening.
In La Boca, children begin to wake,
and someone takes my picture

as I sit in the pale yellow light of *La Poesia*.
I head to Tigre, to walk the riverbanks,
amid the houseboats and jungle of the Paraná Delta.

I take a semi-cama to Rosario
and stand by the riverbank eating empanadas.
The streets are bereft of tourists,

bereft. I take another semi-cama
to Purmamarca, and Tilcara, and Salta, and Jujuy.
Huddled against the evening in a placid square,

I watch an entire town play bingo.
Leading his llama through settling dust, a man sells
Aguayo. Everyone arrives to take in the air,

but I must be on my way.
The bus climbs silently; the frozen Andes,
and cacti slide down the hill.

The moon leans against a cloud
like a man in a black leather jacket, smoking.
Now, I am moving North, into the thin air of the Andes,

towards the border of Bolivia.
I understand why I was told to come here:
the border is a magnet that attracts

the unreconstructed traveller;
it repels in equal measure.
The mercury plummets and I think of continuing.

I offer the young soldier my passport.
He hands it back, but takes someone else away.
My compass needle spins uncertainly,

then lies still. This is a point
beyond magnetism. And we continue,
upward, into mist.

Meseta

Remember the dust-dry death-pits of the *pueblo*
where we walked for hours, with nothing to do?

We had time, then, to plan the long vacation.
You lay on an Inca altar in the sun, a scapegoat

for your picture. I stood in the small doorway
of some ancient crypt, thinking, *They buried their dead—*

the mummified remains of Atacama—inside the pukara,
near to their apartments of adobe. Keep the living close,

and the dead closer; this is the message. It rings out,
cold and true, announcing the edge of an empire

under siege, as empires always are. Our guide
took us up the mountain, pointing out painted rocks

and saying, *pueblo, pueblo, pueblo.* I remember thinking
those words could mean anything: town, people, nation, or

the simple desire for society in the vast solitude of the meseta.
Maybe everything will one day return to desert:

water become silt, leaves thinning out to thorn,
life, a windowless room and a low, stone door.

A case of ceremony and burial, keeping watch
over clouds, river and stone. Handling dust with care.

Salta e Jujuy

I spend most of my time trying not to think
of the daily news, streaming now like a river in spate
declaring, *all rivers have run dry.*

I think instead about a hike in Purmamarca
crossing an iron bridge to set my stone on the cairn
and staring at the dust-dry Rio Grande.

Moving on, towards the *Cerro de los Siete Colores*
I sit and gaze at bands of colour,
striating stone like psychedelia.

Later, I will see a man with his small pony
buying cloths of braided colour in the square.
I will look at the llamas and listen to the evening bells.

Here villagers welcome the dusk together,
taking in the brisk air of the *Quebrada de Humahuaca.*
The dust becomes buildings —

and Bolivian soldiers, no more than boys,
board night-buses to check the passports
of sleeping passengers.

In Tilcara, the *pukaras* of the Incas are empty:
lo siento — I am sorry — *por favor* — please —
with these poor words, somehow we make our way.

Atatürk

~ Atatürk Airport, 28 June, 2016

Something in the air: signals, shrapnel, remnants of the Ottoman Empire.

I felt this was a place through which countless generations had travelled, such that the stranger had become an expected quality of the place itself.

I sensed hospitality and ease, something old-world, mood-sensitive and appreciative of quiet pleasure: a history of travelers, a sensuous history, alert to the bittersweet aftertaste of seduction and departure, sweets and spice, opiates from the Silk Road.

I imagined markets for trade, games of cards and dice in narrow alleyways, carpets, cargo, dominoes, spaces where one might lose money and time.

I gazed out through partitions of glass and mortar, smoking my cigarette, listening to the whispered voices of other passengers, world travelers.

The blood was still being washed from the runway.

For John Ashbery

We are in Parmigianino's studio,
heavy with vapours of oil,
and turpentine-soaked cloth,
decorated with paintbrushes
in jars of clouded water.

Outside, Rome is sacked again,
and the Mannerist chapter
of the Florentine underground
meet in the charnel house
to chart the unchartable future.

Intrigues haunt the shores
of our lacustrine imaginations
and are made real, now,
with such incredible speed
that there is nowhere left to travel.

But do we miss the element
of surprise, the alchemical
chimera that excites
and disturbs in unequal measure?
What say you, Girolamo?

The little man of Parma steps forth
from the shadowed recess.
He makes the sign of his conspirators,
brushing his hand through the flame
of a candle waxing a skull.

Who knows what happened next?

Who visited them?

Skogsägarna Mellanskog ek För

~ *Uppsala, Sweden*

Lacking sense, having nothing to do but wait,
I left the *Hotel Clarion* and walked

down, to the *Fyris*, crossing the footbridge
near the ice-cream stand, and turning down,

like an apostrophe, toward the *Stadsrädgården*.
The path was clean and empty and I heard

my footsteps falling through the forest,
mid-summer falling through the emerald canopy.

I followed the river, following another
solitary walker, heading out of town.

In a weird clearing, I found a tree house, fallen
from its high perch, fallen into a witchcraft

of splintered sticks. I moved on, unperturbed —
no one arrived to hear the forest breathing.

Resting awhile in a shallow delay beside the river,
I saw a yellow rain boot lost to the river's silt,

and Pepsi-Cola cans glittering in grass grown long;
grown into that which I had always called *meadow*.

I moved on, after the call of invisible birds
calling from the castle.

Acknowledgements

Thanks are due to the editors of the following journals in whose pages versions of some of these poems first appeared: *Imago, New Contrast: The South African Literary Journal* and *The Johannesburg Review of Books*.

For their advice, conversation, and support, thanks are also due to my parents, Dennis and Linda, Peter Anderson, Michèle Betty, Stephen James, Sophy Kohler, Rustum Kozain, Jennifer Malec, and Stephen Watson, a mentor and friend who broadened my poetic horizons and deepened my appreciation for poetry. He is sorely missed.

Simon van Schalkwyk

Notes on Epigraphs/Quotations

Phrases, epigraphs and quotations have been used, sometimes with, and sometimes without, acknowledgement from the following sources:

Page 12

it is an old egotist
dreaming of the blue ghosts
of kingfishers

Hope Mirrlees, *Paris. A Poem*, p.14 (Paradise Road, Richmond: Hogarth Press, 1919) http://hopemirrlees.com/texts/Paris_Hope_Mirrlees_1920.pdf

Permission to cite this quotation has been gratefully obtained with the kind permission of Carcanet Press, Manchester, United Kingdom.

Page 28

the land of America
was found by the Merchants of Bristow
in a shippe of Bristowe, called the Mathew

John Cabot quoted in G. E. Weare, *Cabot's Discovery of North America*, p.116 (London: John Mcqueen, 1897) https://books.google.co.za/books?id_IEMzA QAAMAAJ& printsec=frontcover&source=gbs_ge_summary_r&cad=0#v= onepage&q&f=false

*

a trail … inland,
a fire … and … a stick half a yard long pierced at both ends
carved and painted with brazil.

'The John Day Letter' reproduced in J. A. Williamson, *The Cabot Voyages and Bristol Discovery Under Henry VII,* pp. 212–214 (Cambridge University Press, 1962)

Page 29

The reader will often see a particular word, idea or image lifting the latch on the next

Stephen James 'Introduction' in *The Tabla Book of New Verse,* p. XXX (Bristol: Tabla, 2004)

Page 45

The poem 'Curiosity CLXXV' creatively incorporates material from the following found source:

Henk Rossouw, 'Love Letter to a University' in *The Chronicle of Higher Education*, p. 6 (17 December 2004) http://frithalangerman.com/wp-content/uploads/2004/02/Chronicle-of-Higher-Education-Dec-17-2004_small.pdf

Page 51

It is only through personal contact that one can get a few glimpses into the hidden depths of the primitive and childlike yet rich soul of the native, and this soul is what I try to reflect in my pictures.

Irma Stern, 'My Exotic Models', *The Cape Argus* (3 April 1926)

*

The magnet of exotica …

Arthur Nortje , *Dead Roots*, p. 104 (London: Heinemann, 1973)

*

brought in straight from the sea,
huge skites, small vivid-blue fish
with yellow stripes, silvery kinds,
red roman, enormous lobsters,
as made of turquoise matrix,
phantastic huge turtles –
all come out of the tropical sea

Irma Stern, *Zanzibar*, p. 21 (Pretoria: Van Schaik, 1948)

Page 66

small floral souls raised out
of antique vases

Rainer Maria Rilke quoted by Musée Rodin in 'Assemblage: Despairing Youth and Child Ugolino Around Vase' http://www.musee-rodin.fr/en/collections/sculptures/assemblage-despairing-youth-and-child-ugolino-around-vase

The simple desire for society in the vast solitude of the meseta

Richard A. Fletcher, *Saint James's Catapult: The Life and Times of Diego Gelmírez of Santiago de Compostela* (Oxford: Oxford University Press, 1984)

OTHER WORKS IN THE DRYAD PRESS LIVING POETS SERIES

AVAILABLE NOW

The Mountain Behind the House, Kobus Moolman
In Praise of Hotel Rooms, Fiona Zerbst
catalien, Oliver Findlay Price
Allegories of the Everyday, Brian Walter
Otherwise Occupied, Sally Ann Murray
Landscapes of Light and Loss, Stephen Symons
An Unobtrusive Vice, Tony Ullyatt
A Private Audience, Beverly Rycroft
Metaphysical Balm, Michèle Betty

FORTHCOMING IN 2021

Palimpsests, Chris Mann
Dark Horse, Michèle Betty

OTHER WORKS BY DRYAD PRESS (PTY) LTD

River Willows: Senryū from Lockdown, Tony Ullyatt
missing, Beverly Rycroft
The Coroner's Wife: Poems in Translation, Joan Hambidge
Unearthed: A Selection of the Best Poems of 2016, edited by Joan Hambidge
and Michèle Betty

Available in South Africa online at www.dryadpress.co.za
from better bookstores and internationally from African Books Collective
(www.africanbookscollective.com)

Printed in the United States
by Baker & Taylor Publisher Services